GOSPEL STC

THE O.G. INFLUENCER

FOR GEN Z

Contents

Introduction

Yo, what's good, Gen Z? Strap in 'cause you're about to catch all the holy tea with "The OG Influencer: Gospel Stories For Gen Z" Why did we cook up this book? Simple: we're serving the age-old stories of the Bible in a language that's not just fresh AF but also speaks directly to you—the Snapchat, TikTok-loving squad that's shaping the future.

Here's the lowdown: The Bible? It's been around. Like, been translated into mad languages because let's be real, not everyone's vibing on ancient Greek or Hebrew. So, we thought, why not translate these epic tales into Gen Z speak? This isn't about changing the game; it's about dropping Jesus' wisdom, miracles, and parables in a way that doesn't have you snoozing. We're keeping it 100, making these stories accessible and relatable while throwing in enough memes and slang to keep you hooked, no cap.

This book is like Jesus himself slid into your DMs with parables and sermons that slap harder than a TikTok dance challenge. It's for those who say, "I can't even" when faced with old-school text but will stay up till 3 AM binge-watching series or scrolling feeds. We're here to make sure that when it comes to the Big J (yeah, that's Jesus), you're all caught up, fully engaged, and maybe even stoked about spirituality.

Ain't here to throw shade or preach: Just so we're clear, this rewrite isn't about being sacrilegious or clowning on sacred texts. It's about inclusivity and sparking interest in a generation that might feel the OG scripture doesn't resonate with them. The Bible has hit remixes in all sorts of styles;

consider this another remix for those who speak in memes, tweets, and snaps.

So, whether you're here to get those spiritual gains, curious about the buzz around JC, or just in it for the LOLs, "The OG Influencer: Gospel Stories For Gen Z" promises to be a lit journey through the Gospels. You'll see Jesus turning water into the best wine at the party, serving up major truths, and doing the most to show love and light without ever being basic.

Get ready to see the miracles, feel the drama, and maybe, just maybe, get a little moved by the dude who changed the world long before viral was a thing. Let's get it!

CHAPTER 1
Origin Vibes: The Early Years of Jesus

1.1 "Litmas": The Ultimate Glow-Up of Bethlehem

Once upon a vibe in Nazareth, Mary was just chillin', keeping it 100%, when out of the blue, Angel Gabriel slides into her space with a message that's straight fire. Gabriel was like, "Yo, Mary, you're about to level up big time." And Mary was like, "OMG, no cap?" And Gabriel was all, "No cap, you're gonna have the Son of God." Mary was shook, "But um, since I still have my v-card will everyone get that I didn't step out on Joseph?"

Gabriel nods, "Yup, it's all divine plan. No cap, you're still the OG virtuous queen." Mary breathes a sigh of relief, "Phew, 'cause I didn't want to have to clap back at the whole town gossiping. Bet, let's do this."

So Joseph, being the real MVP and not a simp, stood by Mary even though he was kinda salty at first because, you know, the situation was mad sus. But after a divine dream, he was all in, supporting his bae.

So here's the tea: There's a census, and everyone's gotta head back to their hometowns. Mary and Joseph hit the road to Bethlehem, but it's so packed, it's giving Coachella vibes. Every spot's taken, and they end up crashing in a stable. Talk about a rustic-chic vibe check!

Then, BOOM! Baby Jesus was born. Mary was like, "He's such a whole meal!" They wrapped him in some swaddling clothes, and baby Jesus was straight chilling in a manger, serving major glow-up vibes from minute one.

Word got out, and these shepherds rolled up. They were just in the fields, minding their own business when an angel squad popped up like, "Eyyy, we've got some tea! The Savior is born, and it's straight fire!" The shepherds were hyped. They left their sheep on read and swooped over to see baby Jesus, and they were not disappointed. It was giving very much "miracle" vibes.

Meanwhile, these wise men caught wind of the birth through some cosmic, boujee star that was basically the ancient GPS. They packed some dank gifts—gold, frankincense, and myrrh (because what baby doesn't want myrrh, amirite?)—and followed the star, which led them right to Jesus. They rolled up and were all, "Yaas, king!" paying homage and dropping gifts like it was a hot collab drop.

So, there you have it. Jesus's birth was the event of the century, no cap. It had angels, shepherds, wise men, gifts, and a star that was literally lit. And that, fam, is how you tell the Nativity story with some Gen Z sparkle. Wig, totally flown!

1.2 Temple Vibes: The Debut Drop of Baby Jesus

So, Joseph and Mary are vibing with their new bundle of joy, Baby Jesus, and they figure it's time to hit up the Jerusalem scene for the ultimate baby debut. They're lowkey excited but highkey nervous because presenting your kid in the temple is the ancient world's version of an influencer's first post-baby pic—gotta make it count.

They roll into the temple, and it's buzzing harder than a beehive on a hot day. People everywhere, but they've got their eyes on the prize. Joseph's looking fresh, Mary's all glowed up, and Baby Jesus? He's chilling like he owns the place because, well, he kinda does.

Enter Simeon, the hype man of the Holy. This dude's been waiting on the Messiah like it's the drop of the century—like waiting for the PS5 restock. He sees Jesus and basically yeets across the room. He grabs Jesus and is like, "Big bet! This kid is everything. Now I can ghost in peace, 'cause I've seen the squad's future captain."

Then, out of nowhere, Anna, the temple's resident tea-spiller and prophetess, makes her entrance. She's been in the temple game longer than anyone, fasting and praying like it's her job (because it is). She clocks Baby Jesus and immediately starts gassing him up to everyone. "Y'all, this kiddo is the truth. He's the playlist everyone's gonna have on repeat!"

The temple's now popping off like a Friday night, and Mary and Joseph are trying to keep up. They do their thing, dropping their offering in the temple Venmo—two pigeons, keeping it humble yet classy.

As they wrap up the divine meet-and-greet, Mary's storing all these crazy moments in her mental Snapchat, knowing these memories are gonna be worth a fortune in likes and prayers. They head out, Baby Jesus in tow, leaving the crowd shook and the temple never the same.

Joseph, turning to Mary as they exit, is like, "Babe, our kid's gonna trend harder than #Blessed. That was wild."

Mary just nods, her mind already on the next viral moment, because when your kid is the GOAT, every day is a new adventure.

1.3 Starstruck: The Ultimate Collab of the Magi and the Messiah

So, picture this: Far off in the VIP section of the East, there's this trio of clout-chasing Wise Men—aka the Magi. These guys aren't just any influencers; they're celestial trend-spotters, always on the lookout for the next big thing. One night, while they're vibing with their telescopes, they spot this ultra-lit star. And it's not just any star; it's spitting straight fire, practically throwing up peace signs in the sky. They're like, "This star is a whole mood, fam. It's gotta be signaling the drop of the century."

The Magi, geared up with their drip—gold, frankincense, myrrh (because who doesn't gift a newborn some luxe resin?)—decide to yeet across deserts and mountains, following the star like it's the season's hottest playlist leading them to the main event. They're traveling in style, maybe on camels, because even their transport's gotta have that exotic flex.

As they trek, they're updating their Insta scrolls and keeping their followers in the loop. #FollowTheStar becomes the trending hashtag, blowing up feeds everywhere. The journey's hype is real.

Finally, they roll up to Jerusalem, and they're all, "Where's the baby king at?" Herod, the current king and chief hater, catches wind of this and he's straight-up salty. He's got zero chill, thinking another king might steal his clout. Herod plays it cool though, hits them with a, "Yo, hit me up with the deets when you find him, so I can come worship too." Spoiler alert: Homie's got zero intentions of worship.

The star leads the Magi to Bethlehem, and it parks right over this humble crib—like, it's giving very much divine Google Maps. They step in and there's baby Jesus. The vibe is immaculate, and their hearts are full. The Wise Men are shook—like, this baby's the real GOAT, no cap. They drop their gifts, which are total bangers, and the collab is peak wholesomeness.

But then, they catch some divine tea in a dream—Herod's plotting some serious shade. So, they decide to ghost him and head home by another route, dodging the drama. #BypassHerod becomes their new travel motto.

And there you have it: The Wise Men, after securing the ultimate link-up with baby Jesus, keep it 100 and dip out, leaving behind a trail of inspiration and some seriously good vibes. They were the original kings of throwing support behind a newborn influencer.

1.4 Escape to Egypt: The Ultimate Ghosting of King Herod

Once upon a vibe in Bethlehem, the holy fam was just starting to settle when Joseph caught some Z's and scored a divine DM in dreamland. Angel pops up like, "Yo, Joe, heads up—Herod's on a salty rampage, hunting for baby Jesus. Time to dip out, stat!"

Joseph snaps awake, adrenaline maxed out. "Aight, we out!" he declares, shaking Mary awake. "Babe, we gotta skirt-skirt!" Mary, still half in dreamland, is like, "Spill the tea, what's going down?" Joseph's all, "No cap, we gotta ghost Bethlehem. Herod's being extra, and it's giving major sus vibes."

They pack the essentials—swaddles, some myrrh ('cause why not keep it boujee?), and hit the road. They're yeeting across the desert, dodging Herod's clout chasers like they're dodging spoilers for the latest Marvel drop. Joseph's navigating by the stars, lowkey wishing Google Maps was a thing, but they manage because celestial GPS never fails.

Mary's there, trying to keep it chill but also kinda freaking out, "OMG, Joseph, are we even going the right way?" Joseph, confident in his star-following skills, is like, "Trust, babe. I've got the celestial co-ords on lock."

Meanwhile, back in Bethlehem, Herod's throwing a fit that's so not chill. Dude's tweeting up a storm, rage-quit style, because he got ghosted so hard. But our holy fam is way ahead, blending in Egypt like pros.

Once in Egypt, they slip into incognito mode. They're hitting up the local markets, Joseph maybe flipping his carpentry skills and turning wood into art 'cause that's how he rolls. Baby Jesus is lowkey being his adorable self, probably inventing new baby trends or something.

Mary's diving into local mom groups, sharing top-tier mom hacks and probably starting a side hustle with her myrrh-infused baby oil. She's serving major mom goals.

Herod's still on his king-sized tantrum, checking his royal Twitter every five minutes, but he's just catching L's. Meanwhile, our fam is all safe, chilling under the radar, catching W's in Egypt, waiting for the all-clear.

And there you have it—the holy family's legendary ghosting of Herod. They didn't just escape; they turned their flight into a stealth mode saga that's straight-up legendary, setting the bar for holy ghostings and divine protections.

1.5 Nazareth Nuances: The Holy Fam's Epic Comeback

So, after ghosting Herod and chilling in Egypt like nomads on a top-secret mission, the holy fam was finally ready to hit up their old digs in Nazareth. It was a major glow-up moment because, let's be real, avoiding a king's wrath is no small feat.

Joseph gets the all-clear in another divine DM — the angel's like, "Yo, Joseph, Herod's out, his crew's done. Time to bounce back home, fam!" Joseph's all, "Bet, let's pack it up!" So they gather their life, which by now is pretty boujee with all the Egyptian threads and trinkets they've collected.

They yeet back to Nazareth, rolling into town like they never dipped. The neighbors are throwing side eyes, whispering, "Weren't they ghosted?" But Mary's just serving looks with baby Jesus, who's no longer just a baby but a whole vibe.

Joseph sets up shop again, turning wood into artisanal masterpieces. He's basically the carpenter version of a hypebeast now, with all these new Egyptian techniques that have the whole town talking. "Joseph's workshop slaps," they say, because his furniture is no cap, the real deal.

Mary, on the flip side, is all about community vibes. She's starting convo chains, spilling tea but keeping it sweet, and sharing all these life hacks she picked up abroad. She's practically an influencer in Nazareth, with other moms looking to her for the 411 on everything from cooking to child-rearing. "Mary's recipes? They're bussin'," the locals tweet.

Little Jesus? He's growing up with these killer storytimes from both worlds. He's got parables from Egypt and miracle vibes brewing. You could say he's the childhood GOAT, gathering his squad of future disciples at like, age 5. He's got this charisma, this heavenly rizz that even the old heads in town can't deny.

As the fam settles in, Nazareth starts feeling less like the backseat and more like the main stage. It's not just a comeback; it's a whole new era. "Nazareth is glowing up," people post, because with the holy fam back, the town's got a new spark.

And that's how the holy fam turned their homecoming into the hottest event in Nazareth, setting up Jesus for his future gigs as the ultimate influencer. It's a mix of divine swag, carpentry clout, and community serve that's got everyone in Nazareth living, laughing, and loving their newfound vibe.

1.6 Temple Takedown: Young Jesus Schools the Scholars

So, check it: The holy fam was in Jerusalem, vibing at the Passover festival, which was basically the Coachella of ancient times— everyone was there. After the fest, Mary and Joseph were ready to bounce back to Nazareth, but lil' Jesus had other plans. He was like, "Imma stay back, catch some wisdom vibes from the temple crew." Only, he didn't drop a pin or send a text, so his parents were clueless.

Three days later, Mary and Joseph are in full panic mode, hitting up every spot in Jerusalem. "This kid's got us on a wild goose chase, fr," Mary's saying, while Joseph's checking every corner like, "Where's this young king at?"

Cut to Jesus, just chilling in the temple, serving straight facts and wisdom to the old heads there. The scholars and teachers are all gathered around him, throwing questions, and Jesus is hitting them back with answers so fire, it's got everyone shook. They're whispering, "Yo, who's this kid? He's spitting straight wisdom with no cap!"

Finally, Mary and Joseph storm into the temple, and Mary's like, "Son, you had us scared AF! Why you gotta do us dirty like that?" Jesus, cool as a cucumber, hits them with, "Why were you searching for me? Didn't you know I had to be in my Father's house, serving up these holy truths?"

Mary and Joseph are kinda stumped because, what can you say to that? But they're also low-key proud because their boy's not just smart; he's divine smart.

So they yeet back to Nazareth, but now everyone's eyes are on Jesus. He's no longer just the carpenter's son; he's the young prodigy who threw down at the temple and had everyone's jaws on the floor.

Jesus keeps it humble, though, respecting his parents and leveling up in wisdom and swag. Nazareth's buzzing, tweets are flying, and Jesus is trending. "#YoungWisdomKing" is popping off because this wasn't just any temple run; it was the Temple Takedown, where young Jesus schooled the scholars and set the stage for what was to come.

1.7 Splash Drop: Jesus' Epic Baptism and Divine Shoutout

So, peep this: After Jesus was out here schooling those temple OGs as a kiddo, He's ready to launch His public clout—like, it's debut time, fam! Cue the hype music, 'cause our main man, Jesus, is about to hit the divine runway.

Enter John the Baptist, the ultimate hypebeast of the wilderness, rocking camel hair and snacking on locusts like they're limited edition snacks. John's not just a weird flex; he's prepping the squad for Jesus' big drop. He's out here in the river, baptizing peeps left and right, telling everyone to clean up their act 'cause something big is about to pop off.

Jesus rolls up to the Jordan, lowkey blending in with the crowd. But, nah, He can't just blend in, right? He steps up, and John's like, "Bro, should be me getting baptized by you, tbh." But Jesus is all about setting that humble example, so he's like, "Nah, fam, let's run it. Gotta keep it 💯 for the prophecy and all that."

So, they're in the water, right? And when Jesus gets dipped and comes up, it's like nature hits the pause button. Sky cracks open, sunlight's beaming like a spotlight—major cinematic vibes. And if that wasn't extra enough, boom, a dove comes cruising down, all graceful and whatnot. It's the Holy Spirit, pulling up in dove form, blessing the scene.

But wait, it gets more lit: A voice thunders from the heavens, booming across the water, "This is my Son, the real deal, in whom I'm mad proud!" Talk about an epic shoutout!

Everyone's jaws? Dropped. Phones out, people probably trying to snap this miracle moment, tweeting, "Just saw Jesus get baptized and it was no cap miraculous! #Blessed #DoveDrop."

Post-baptism, Jesus is all charged up, ready to kick off His mission with that divine co-sign. He's got the drip, the clout, and now, the heavenly thumbs up. It's not just a baptism; it's a divine endorsement. And as Jesus steps out the river, you better believe His follower count started popping off.

And there you have it—**"Splash Drop: Jesus' Epic Baptism and Divine Shoutout"**—where our boy J sets the stage for the ultimate redemption arc, one that's about to turn water into wine, flip tables, and straight-up redefine #Blessed.

CHAPTER 2
Miracle Mixtape: Jesus' Top Chart Hits

Track 1: Water Into That Fine Wine – The Wedding Banger

Alright, let's set the scene. Picture this: Jesus and His crew rolling deep into a wedding party in Cana. Everyone's dressed to the nines, the music's bumping, and the vibes are just immaculate. But then, plot twist—the wine taps run dry. Total buzzkill, right? The guests are starting to whisper, and the hosts are low-key panicking because, let's be real, running out of wine at a wedding is like your playlist ending right when the dance floor gets lit.

Enter Mary, Jesus' mom, who's always tuned in to the needs around her. She catches the vibe and doesn't hesitate to nudge Jesus. She's like, "Son, they're about to write some bad Yelp reviews. Time to flex." Jesus, initially playing it cool, is like, "Mom, it's not my time to hit the stage yet." But Mary, knowing her son's potential to turn up, goes ahead and tells the servants, "Do whatever he tells you." That's trust on a whole new level.

Now, Jesus, seeing the chance to not only save the party but also to set off his public ministry with a major headline, steps up to the plate. He spots six stone water jars, the kind used for ceremonial washing—basically ancient hand sanitizers—and he's got a plan. He tells the servants, "Fill these up with water." And not just a little top-up; we're talking to the brim, make it overflow.

Once the jars are stacked with H2O, Jesus gives the crew a simple instruction, "Now draw some out and take it to the master of the banquet." Imagine being those servants, wondering if this was about to be their last gig. But faith makes them move, and they do just as Jesus says.

The master of the banquet, totally oblivious to the behind-the-scenes miracle, takes a sip of this freshly transformed wine, and his taste buds are shook. This isn't your average wedding wine; it's like something straight out of a VIP cellar. He's so impressed, he pulls aside the bridegroom and throws him a compliment that's music to any host's ears, "Everyone brings out the choice wine first and then the cheaper stuff after guests have had too much. But you? You've saved the best till now."

Boom. Mic drop. Jesus just turned a potential party fail into an epic win. Guests are now sipping on this divine vino, wondering, "Yo, where has this lush juice been hiding?" The mood shifts from worried whispers to cheers and toasts. Jesus, with one smooth move, not only keeps the party popping but also puts His miracle mojo on the map. His rep as a miracle mixer? Sky-high. His squad? Totally hyped. And the wedding guests? They're just getting started.

This miracle wasn't just about turning water into wine; it was about showing that with Jesus, the best is always yet to come. So when you think you're hitting rock bottom, or the party's over, that's when He steps in, turning your plain old water into that fine wine. Party saved, faith restored, and the Jesus hype? Just getting started.

Track 2: Five Loaves, Two Fish – The All-You-Can-Eat Buffet Drop

Imagine this: you're at a festival with a crowd that's 5K strong. The vibes are high, the sun's out, but there's just one glitch—everyone's stomachs are growling, and there's not enough grub to go around. This is the scene where we find Jesus, surrounded by a sea of folks who've been listening to His teachings all day and are now seriously hungry.

In the mix, there's just five loaves and two fish—sounds like someone's modest picnic, right? These aren't just any snacks; they're about to become the centerpiece of the most epic food drop in history. A young kid steps up, lunchbox in hand, and what happens next? Jesus takes this mini meal, looks up to the heavens with a nod, and blesses it. It's showtime.

What comes next is nothing short of miraculous. Jesus starts breaking bread like a chef at a gourmet gala, handing pieces to His disciples to distribute. And here's where it gets wild: the more they give out, the more there seems to be. The baskets keep coming back fuller than when they left. It's like the ultimate buffet, but instead of running out, the food levels are scaling up. People are passing dishes, piling their plates, and munching away. The vibe is electric—everyone's fueling up, and the energy is contagious.

But Jesus isn't just filling bellies; He's making a point about abundance and sharing. With each piece of bread and fish that goes out, He's showing that when you start with generosity, the returns are beyond what you could calculate. It's like, the more you give, the more you get, flipping the script on what it means to have enough.

As the food keeps flowing, the crowd starts to realize this isn't your regular meal. They're part of a moment that's bigger than just feeding a few thousand folks—it's a sign that with Jesus, there's always more than enough to go around. And as the disciples gather twelve baskets of leftovers, it's clear this wasn't just about satisfying hunger; it was a lesson in divine provision.

The crowd is buzzing, everyone's full, not just with food, but with awe. And as they share their #BlessedByTheBread stories, the news of what happened spreads faster than a viral dance challenge. Everyone's tweeting, snapping, sharing—Jesus just hosted the ultimate all-you-can-eat buffet with just a kid's lunch and a prayer.

This miracle isn't just a party trick; it's a message about community, sharing, and the power of faith to turn what's seemingly insufficient into more than enough. So next time you think you're running low—on resources, on energy, on hope—remember the five loaves and two fish. With a little faith and a lot of sharing, you might just find yourself at the heart of your own all-you-can-eat miracle.

Track 3: Storm Stiller – The Wave Crusher

Ever found yourself smack in the middle of chaos, like when you're on a boat and a wild storm decides to crash your cruise? Picture this: Jesus and His crew are just chilling on a boat crossing the Sea of Galilee, vibes are good, the water's calm. But outta nowhere, the weather pulls a 180—sudden squall, waves going sicko mode, boat's rocking like it's trying to win a dance battle. And the disciples? Yeah, they're straight-up losing their minds.

But guess who's snoozing through this aquatic uproar? Jesus, yes, homie was knocked out, catching Z's in the stern on a cushion like it's just another lazy Sunday. Meanwhile, His squad's freaking out, water's splashing in, and the boat's looking more like a bathtub toy in a hurricane than a sturdy vessel.

So, they wake Jesus up, practically yelling, "Bro, you sleepin'? We're about to be fish food!" Imagine the scene: these grown men, seasoned fishermen, scared they're about to caps and it's curtains for them all. But Jesus? He rubs the sleep from His eyes, probably stifles a yawn, and looks around like, "Really, guys?"

Then, with the chill of someone turning down the thermostat, Jesus steps up and is like, "Chill, be still!" Just like that, He commands the wind and the waves with the authority of a boss-level influencer. No shouting, no dramatic gestures, just straight-up tells the storm to sit down and behave. And the sea? It goes from rave-level wild to smoother than a TikTok dance routine in a heartbeat.

The disciples? Their jaws hit the deck. They're looking around, eyes wide, minds blown, asking each other, "Who even is this guy?!" Because one minute they're about to call Davy Jones' locker home, and the next, it's like they're floating on a glass pond. They've seen Jesus do some cool stuff, sure, but controlling nature with just a couple of words? That's next-level.

This moment isn't just about saving their skins; it's a massive flex of divine power. Jesus shows that even the wind and waves are in His followers' playlist, and they gotta hit pause when He says so. It's a lesson for the disciples—and for us, too. No matter how outta control life gets, how overwhelming the chaos, there's a power that can calm any storm, and it's on our side.

So, next time you feel like you're in over your head, remember the Storm Stiller, the Wave Crusher. Jesus didn't just quiet a storm; He showed His crew (and us) that with faith, we could face the roughest seas and not just survive but cruise through with confidence. That's some divine clout that commands nature, no cap.

Track 4: Walk on Water – The Liquid Stroll

Imagine you're chilling by the lakeside when suddenly, you witness the ultimate flex: someone walking on water, no tricks, no illusions, just straight-up strolling on the lake like it's downtown pavement. That's the scene we've got when Jesus decides to take water walking from myth to reality, turning the Sea of Galilee into his personal runway.

So here's the setup: The disciples are out on the boat, middle of the night, and the weather decides to throw a wild party. We're talking waves crashing, wind howling—the kind of storm that makes even seasoned sailors think twice. And these guys are struggling, rowing hard but getting nowhere fast. The vibe? Definitely tense.

Then, out of nowhere, here comes Jesus, making his entrance like the main character in every epic movie ever. He's just casually walking on water, calm as you like, while everything else is going off-script. The disciples are freaking out, thinking they're seeing things. "It's a ghost," they shout, because what else could it be?

But Jesus, ever the chill influencer, calls out, "Chill, it's just me. No need to panic." As if walking on water wasn't enough of a mic drop, He's also totally unfazed by their fear.

Peter, never one to shy away from a challenge, gets hyped and he's like, "Bet, if it's really you, tell me to come to you on the water." And Jesus, probably with a can't-believe-he's-really-going-to-try-this grin, simply says, "Come on then."

So, Peter hops out of the boat and, believe it or not, starts walking on water too. Yep, he's actually doing it—living the miracle, making those #WaterWalkingChallenge dreams come true. But then, he takes a look around, sees the chaos of the storm, and starts to sink. Classic Peter, right?

Just as he's about to become a human submarine, Jesus is there, hand out, catching him. "You of little faith," He says, "why did you doubt?" And just like that, they're back in the boat, the storm dies down, and everyone's jaws are on the deck. The disciples are mind-blown, worshiping Jesus, saying, "Truly, you are the Son of God." Because who else could turn a storm into a stroll?

This isn't just a party trick; it's a full-blown demonstration of faith and power. Jesus shows that, with enough belief, you can not only face your storms but walk right over them. And for Peter? It's a quick lesson in keeping your eyes on the prize (or in this case, the Savior) rather than the chaos around you.

So next time life throws you into rough waters, remember the liquid stroll. Whether you're walking on water or just trying to stay afloat, keeping your focus on faith can turn panic into peace and fear into something fantastic.

Track 5: Sight for Sore Eyes – The Vision Restorer

Let's dive into a story where vision is more than just sight—it's about revelation and transformation. In a dusty town, as word spreads of a man named Jesus whose touch could mend the broken and restore the impossible, two blind men find themselves stirred by a hope they hadn't felt in years. These men, accustomed to darkness, hear tales of Jesus, the light-bringer, and decide it's time to see for themselves—literally.

As they learn Jesus is nearby, they don't sit back; instead, they pursue Him, their voices echoing through the streets, "Son of David, have mercy on us!" Their call is a powerful testament to their belief in Jesus' lineage and His divine authority. It's not just a shout for help; it's an acknowledgment of Jesus as the Messiah, a plea steeped in faith.

When Jesus hears them, He doesn't immediately respond with miracles as He often does. Instead, He engages them in a crucial dialogue, pulling them aside to ask, "Do you believe that I am able to do this?" This question isn't casual; it's central to their healing, probing the depth of their faith and readiness to have their lives changed forever.

With firm conviction, they respond, "Yes, Lord," a simple yet profound affirmation of their trust and belief. Moved by their faith, Jesus touches their eyes. In that moment, the miraculous occurs—not just the restoration of sight, but the granting of a vision that had previously been beyond reach. Suddenly, they see the world in vibrant clarity, witnessing the beauty of creation and the face of their healer.

Though Jesus instructs them to keep this miracle quiet, their excitement and awe are too great to contain. They become heralds of the miracle, spreading the word far and wide, unable to keep silent about the gift they have received. Their story illustrates not just a physical healing, but a spiritual awakening.

This tale of the two men who regained their sight is a vivid reminder of the transformative power of faith and the impact of Jesus' touch. It challenges us to consider what we are seeking from Jesus and encourages us to come to Him with boldness and conviction, ready for the changes He can bring into our lives. It's not merely about what we want to see, but how we choose to look at the world once our vision is restored.

CHAPTER 3
Squad Goals: Disciples Doing the Most

3.1 Peter: The Rockstar

Starting off strong with Peter, the OG disciple. Once a simple fisherman, Peter's life got flipped-turned upside down when Jesus was like, "Come follow me, and I'll make you a fisher of men." Known for his bold, sometimes brash energy, Peter was always ready to dive headfirst, whether walking on water (kinda) or chopping off ears in Jesus' defense. When the clout of being Jesus' right-hand man hit, Peter had to navigate the waves of fame, even slipping up by denying Jesus thrice. But post-resurrection, he leveled up, leading the early church and becoming the rock Jesus always believed he could be.

3.2 John: The VIP Behind-the-Scenes

John, the beloved, was all about that love life—not in the way you think, but in preaching love as Jesus' core message. This dude was like Jesus' personal scribe, writing down the tea and keeping records that would turn into the 'Book of John.' Despite the fame, John stayed low-key, focusing on the squad's mission and taking care of biz, like looking after Jesus' mom post-crucifixion. His role? Keep the love and truth of Jesus' message alive through his gospel and letters.

3.3 Matthew: From Tax Collector to Treasurer

Talk about a career switch—Matthew went from tax collector (read: not the crowd's favorite) to a key player in Jesus' squad. His background in finance made him the unofficial treasurer, managing those donation drops and food funds. But Matthew's glow-up was about shedding his old, corrupt life for a spot in history as one of the gospel writers. His account gave us the receipts on Jesus' life, serving as a bridge between Jewish traditions and the new school Jesus was preaching.

3.4 Thomas: The Doubt Influencer

Thomas, oh Thomas, the guy who made doubting cool long before it was a thing. Known for questioning Jesus' resurrection until he could drop a fact-check, Thomas was all about getting to the truth. His doubts made him super relatable, showing the world that faith isn't about blind follows; it's okay to seek proof. Once convinced, Thomas was all-in, bringing the Jesus brand to new markets, even as far as India.

3.5 Judas: The Betrayal Clickbait

No squad is complete without a little drama, and Judas brought it in spades. The treasurer with a taste for the finer things, he managed the money but slipped a few coins into his own pockets. His ultimate clickbait moment? Betraying Jesus for 30 silver pieces—a move that would haunt his legacy forever. Judas' story is a cautionary tale of what happens when fame, fortune, and greed overshadow the mission.

CHAPTER 4
High-Key Ministry: Sermons that Broke the Internet

4.1 The Sermon on the Mount: Blessed Be the Tweets

So, here's the scene: Jesus just yeets up this hill, no backstage passes needed, 'cause this gig is open access. The crowd is buzzing, everyone's squeezing in for a front-row experience, 'cause word on the street is Jesus drops truth bombs that hit different.

He starts rolling out these beatitudes, and man, it's like He's crafting the sickest tweet thread ever. First up, He's all, "Blessed are the poor in spirit," and it's clear He's not just talking money; it's about those feeling low-key lost or spiritually bankrupt—big mood. He's saying, "Y'all got VIP passes to the kingdom of heaven." Mind. Blown.

Then Jesus keeps the bangers coming. "Blessed are those who mourn, for they will be comforted." It's like He's reaching out to everyone's pain posts, hitting them with a comfort follow. Every beatitude, from the meek scoring the earth as their inheritance to the peacemakers getting called God's children, is a total mic-drop moment. He's redefining blessed—not about being on top of your game or flooding feeds with success selfies, but finding strength and hope in the struggle.

"Blessed are the pure in heart, for they will see God." That's Jesus saying clean hearts see clearer. No filters needed, just 100% authentic vibes.

And don't even get me started on "Blessed are those who are persecuted because of righteousness, for theirs is the kingdom of heaven." Jesus is straight-up calling out to everyone catching heat for doing right, telling them their struggle has got an epic payoff.

This sermon? It wasn't just comforting. It was revolutionary, flipping the script on what it means to be blessed. Jesus wasn't here to play; He was here to change the game. Each beatitude slaps harder than a viral meme, spotlighting the underdogs, the overlooked, and the straight-up real ones.

By the time Jesus wraps, the crowd's not just moved; they're transformed. They came for a sermon but left with a blueprint for beating life at its own game. Jesus showed that real blessings aren't about clout or coins; they're about being grounded in the real stuff—spirit, mourning, meekness, righteousness. It's about being #blessed in ways that hashtags can't even capture.

So yeah, "The Sermon on the Mount" wasn't just a talk. It was Jesus laying down the ultimate thread, a masterclass in what it really means to vibe with the kingdom vibes. No cap, just divine truth, one blessed tweet at a time.

4.2 The Salt of the Earth: Stay Seasoned, Fam

Alright, let's dial in! Next on the playlist, Jesus is about to spill some major truth tea about being the "salt of the earth." This isn't just about adding a little flavor to your foodie posts; it's deep, like seasoning your whole life with purpose.

Jesus pops off with this iconic line: "You are the salt of the earth." But, He's quick to drop a reality check. "But if salt loses its saltiness, how can it be made salty again?" That's Jesus getting all up in our grill with the real talk. He's not here to sugarcoat. If you lose your edge, your essence, what's left? You're basically basic, and who's here for that?

He's throwing this challenge to everyone, especially the influencers of His day – the big dogs, the high-key moral compasses. Jesus is like, "Listen up, don't just blend into the background. Stand out. Keep it authentic." It's a whole vibe about maintaining your impact, not just for the 'Gram but in the grand scheme of things.

This is where Jesus gets real about staying woke. Not just awake, but aware, alive to the needs around you. He's saying be that essential spice, not just for taste but for preservation. Back in the day, salt wasn't just for kicks; it kept things from going bad, it was life-preserving. So, Jesus is essentially calling His crew to be life-preservers in a world that's easy to let things rot spiritually and morally.

He wraps this up with a killer call to action, "Let your light shine before others, that they may see your good deeds and glorify your

Father in heaven." It's like, don't just live; illuminate. Shine bright, make a difference, flex that inner goodness for the world to see. It's about being so authentically you that you can't help but light up the darkest corners of the feed and beyond.

So, yeah, being the salt of the earth? It's about keeping that signature flavor in all you do—staying seasoned, fam. It's about living out loud, being real in your actions, and not just for the applause or the follows. Salt preserves, enhances, and makes a difference—be that salt. Keep it 100, sprinkle that good-good everywhere you go, and watch how you season the world with your epic presence and actions. Stay salty, my friends, in all the right ways.

4.3 Light of the World: Shine Bright, Shine Far

Alright, fam, let's glow up! Jesus isn't just preaching; He's straight-up dropping lifestyle hacks. Next on His sermon tour, He hits us with this blazing concept: "You are the light of the world." Yeah, that's right—you! He's all about shining bright, not just for the clout but to light up the whole game.

Peep this scenario: Jesus says, imagine you're a city perched up on a hill. Are you gonna throw a blackout curtain over that vibe? Heck no! You're gonna blaze up the night, visible for miles, like the sickest festival lights. And if you're a lamp, you're not hiding under the bed like last season's fashion no-no. Nah, you're up on a stand, glowing for the whole room, serving major lumens.

Jesus is laying down this cosmic challenge: "Let your light shine before others." It's like, don't hoard that glow for yourself. Spread it around. Illuminate paths, guide the lost, and bring warmth to the cold spots of this world. When you flex those good deeds, it's not just about lighting up your feed with feel-good content; it's about leading the way so others can vibe on that frequency too.

And here's the kicker: When you light it up with acts of kindness, compassion, and justice, you're not just scoring earthly likes; you're making the Big Boss upstairs proud. That's right, your heavenly Father is getting all the props because you chose to shine your light instead of dimming down under the weight of the world.

So, what's the takeaway? Don't just be a follower, be a beacon.

Whether you're rocking center stage or shining from the sidelines, your light has power. Power to brighten, to reveal, to inspire. Jesus is calling you not just to turn on the switch, but to be the switch. Be that beam that cuts through the darkest nights and leads ships safely to shore.

In the grand story of life, everyone can be a lighthouse, a city on a hill, a lamp on a stand—whatever fits your style. But the goal remains the same: Shine so hard that your light reaches the farthest corners of the earth, and your deeds become the talk of the heavens. Let's get it, light squad—shine bright, shine far, and keep it lit!

4.4 The Lord's Prayer: Viral Vibe Check

Alright, listen up! We're about to deep dive into the ultimate spiritual blueprint—The Lord's Prayer. This isn't just your regular holy recital; it's the masterclass in vibing with the divine. When Jesus shared this prayer, it was like dropping a viral hit that's still streaming strong centuries later.

Here's how Jesus crafts this spiritual connect: "Our Father in heaven, hallowed be your name." This line hits different. It's about giving props to the ultimate Creator, recognizing His place way above the cloud level—major respect where it's due. It's personal yet powerful, like tagging the CEO directly in your life's updates.

Next up, Jesus rolls out, "Your kingdom come, Your will be done, on earth as it is in heaven." It's about syncing up with the divine strategy, hoping to mirror that heavenly peace and order right here on the ground. Think of it as aligning your daily drops with the universe's major releases—getting that alignment just right.

Moving on, He says, "Give us today our daily bread." This part's about keeping your needs in check, ensuring you're asking for the essentials to keep you hustling through the day—not just feasting on wants. It's a daily check-in, ensuring you stay nourished and energized, both in body and spirit.

"Forgive us our debts, as we also have forgiven our debtors," Jesus teaches next. This is the cleanse your feed desperately needs—letting go of grudges and bad vibes to keep your soul's timeline clean. It's a mutual thing; you get what you give. Forgive to keep your own vibe pure and uncluttered.

Jesus closes with, "And lead us not into temptation, but deliver us from the evil one." It's like saying, "Keep us on the right track, away from the trolls and the toxicity." In the vast feed of life, it's about skipping the clickbait that could drag you down, choosing paths that elevate.

To cap it off, The Lord's Prayer isn't just about sending up words; it's about tuning into a frequency that transcends the usual noise. It's a daily reminder to keep it real, keep it respectful, and keep it aligned with the heavens. It's not just about saying the words; it's about living them, making them the background music to your everyday hustle.

Remember, this prayer isn't about gaining followers or likes; it's about maintaining a direct line to the One who matters most. It's the OG of all prayers, setting the tone for a life well-lived and a soul well-aligned. Keep this prayer in your daily rotation and watch how it transforms not just your moments but your entire mindset. Stay connected, stay grounded, and keep the divine vibes flowing!

4.5 Love Your Enemies: The Ultimate Clapback

Alright, strap in, 'cause we're about to unpack one of the most fire tweets Jesus ever dropped. When He said, "Love your enemies and pray for those who persecute you," He wasn't just throwing shade; He was launching the ultimate counter-attack against the hate-hype culture. This isn't your typical "kill 'em with kindness" move; it's about leveling up to radical love that snaps the chain of clapbacks and cancels.

Imagine this: You're scrolling through your feed, and someone drops a toxic comment, trying to start a flame war. The old-school playbook says to hit back harder, right? But here's Jesus, flipping the script like He's rewriting the rules of the game. He's like, "Drop a heart react on that hate. Pray for them. Show love that's so extra, it breaks the algorithm of negativity." It's like responding to a troll with a positivity bomb that leaves them and everyone else shook.

Jesus hits them with, "If you love only those who love you, what reward is there in that?" That's Jesus asking why you'd want to play on easy mode, where everyone loves their fans but blocks the haters. He's challenging everyone to boss up to hardcore mode, where you love the haters too. It's about being so secure in your vibes that you can share them even with your online enemies.

This command is about disrupting the feed of vengeance and spite that can go viral in the worst way. It's about crafting a legacy of vibes so resilient that they turn haters into heart-reactors. By loving those who come at you, you're not just avoiding drama; you're setting a new trend in how conflicts are handled.

Jesus is basically the community manager of humanity, showing how to handle trolls without becoming one. "Love your enemies" isn't just good advice; it's a game-changer that transforms potential beef into peace offerings. This approach doesn't just level up your personal peace stats; it upgrades the whole community's vibe.

So next time you catch some heat in your notifications, remember: Jesus already dropped the ultimate clapback strategy. Love hits harder than any hate could. It's the flex that keeps on flexing, the comment that everyone remembers not because it stung, but because it healed. Keep that radical love on tap, and watch as it remixes the worst into the best. That's not just winning; that's winning differently.

4.6 The Parable of the Good Samaritan: Love Without Limits

Queue up the next viral hit from Jesus' storytime sessions, 'cause this one's about to trend across all your feeds. Picture this: a dude gets jumped on a dusty road, left all kinds of wrecked and roadside. Enter stage left and right, a priest and a Levite—two high-profile community figures you'd expect to jump into action, right? Wrong. They peep the scene, then hit the nope button, crossing to the other side. Major pass. Not a good look, guys.

But hold up, plot twist incoming. Along comes a Samaritan, and not just any Samaritan—the kind folks usually side-eye due to all the bad blood and beef between communities. What does he do? He doesn't just scroll past; he stops, swoops in, and serves some serious first-aid goals. This Samaritan isn't playing; he's about that action. He patches the guy up, tosses him on his own ride, takes him to an inn, and even flips the bill for the stay. Talk about going all out!

Jesus drops this tale not just for the likes or the shares but to shake up the status quo on who qualifies as a neighbor. It's a savage callout against ethnic profiling and a radical rally for humanity. The message? Real neighbors don't calculate kindness based on clout or color; they see a need, and they fill it. No hesitations, no conditions, no limits.

This parable went viral because it wasn't just a story; it was a challenge—a challenge to be a neighbor, not a bystander. It's easy to double-tap a support post or send a heart emoji, but stepping into the messiness of real-life crises? That's where true character is tested. Jesus is asking everyone to level up, to transform from passive scrollers into active helpers, from those who watch to those who act.

So next time you're cruising through your daily routine and you spot someone taking hits—whether IRL or online—remember the Good Samaritan. Don't just pass by; be that unexpected hero. Break down barriers, cross those roads, and bring the help you'd hope to find if you were in the ditch. That's neighborly love without limits, and it's how you truly trend in the kingdom of heaven. Stay woke, stay compassionate, and stay ready to serve, because love—real love— knows no boundaries.

CHAPTER 5
Prelude to the Passion

5.1 The Tension Builds

Yo, so here's the lowdown: Jerusalem was buzzing, not just with the usual hustle and bustle, but with some serious drama brewing in the streets and shadows. Jesus, having just rolled up with His squad for Passover, was dropping truth bombs left and right—parables and sermons that were not just stirring the pot, but basically flipping it over.

As He's weaving through the city, dropping these divine truth bombs, the high priests and the religious bigwigs are starting to catch major feels—not the good kind. They're watching their influence drip away as this carpenter from Nazareth is gathering followers like He's headlining Coachella. Every miracle, every parable, He's like trending #1 on the Jerusalem feed, and these temple elites? They're not having it. It's giving very much threatened vibes.

Meanwhile, Jesus is all calm and collected, riding that wave of destiny like He's got GPS coordinates straight from heaven. But His crew? They're sort of catching the tension, whispering among themselves, side-eyeing the Pharisees who are practically breathing fire every time Jesus lays down another spiritual smackdown.

It's getting spicy in Jerusalem, and not just because of the market's herbs. Every corner they turn, there's whispers, side glances, and a noticeable uptick in shady characters skulking around. The air is thick, not just with dust and donkey smells, but with anticipation of something big about to pop off. Everyone's on edge, waiting for the next move in this celestial chess game, wondering who's gonna make the next play.

So, as Passover gets into full swing, and the city swells with pilgrims, Jesus is dropping more and more of these spiritual mic drops. It's like every word He says is a tweet storm stirring up the masses. And the higher-ups? They're plotting, scheming, their minds racing faster than a chariot at the Hippodrome. They're desperate to cancel Jesus before He can go viral once more. But little do they know, they're just extras in a much bigger story that's about to hit its climactic plot twist.

5.2 The Betrayal

Now, let's spill the tea on the ultimate clout chaser gone wrong—Judas Iscariot. This dude was part of Jesus' inner circle, one of the squad, but he was about to flip the script in the most dramatic way. While Jesus was out there gaining followers, performing miracles, and basically being the ancient world's trendsetter, Judas was getting a little salty about how things were going down.

Here's the sitch: Judas wasn't just vibing with the whole 'serve and save' game plan. Nah, he was eyeing those donation boxes and feeling some type of way about Jesus flipping tables instead of stacking coins. So when the temple bigwigs slid into his DMs with an offer loaded with silver—thirty pieces, to be exact—Judas thought it was his time to secure the bag. Talk about a low-key disaster waiting to happen.

The plan? A simple emoji of a kiss. Yeah, Judas was going to use a kiss to tag Jesus for the authorities. No cap, it was all set for the darkest meet-up in history. So, fast forward to the Garden of Gethsemane, Jesus is deep in His feels, praying hard under the olive trees, downloading some serious heavenly guidance. He knew the vibes were off, and things were about to get real.

Enter Judas, rolling up with the chief priests' squad, all geared up like they're about to drop the hottest arrest of the year. And Judas? He's leading the pack, about to drop the most infamous double-cross. He walks up to Jesus, says "Rabbi!" and plants that kiss. It wasn't just a kiss, though; it was the signal, the moment everything changed.

The disciples? They're shook, watching this Snapchat-worthy betrayal go down, and suddenly, it's swords out, chaos ensues—Peter even swings his blade, turning the scene into a literal ear-cutting event. But Jesus, ever the peacekeeper, is like, "Nah, let's keep it chill," healing the dude and basically showing once again why He's the GOAT.

And just like that, with a kiss, Judas trades his disciple badge for infamy. It's a vibe check that goes horribly wrong, setting off a chain of events that's about to shake history. Betrayal, silver, and a kiss—more drama than any reality TV, and trust, the fallout was about to be biblical.

5.3 The Trial: The Ultimate Cancel Culture Showdown

Alright, so after Judas' major betrayal flex, Jesus was thrown into the lion's den of ancient justice, and fam, it was more like being passed around in a game of hot potato between Pilate and Herod. The stakes? Higher than your favorite influencer's follower count during a viral moment.

First up, Jesus got dragged before Pilate, the Roman big boss in town. Pilate's crib, the praetorium, was the stage for what was less a trial and more of a high-key interrogation session. But here's the tea: Pilate wasn't really feeling the whole condemning vibe. He peeped the situation, listened to Jesus (who was all zen and barely clapping back), and was like, "This dude? Really? What's the charge? Being too woke?"

But the crowd was thirsty for drama. They were spamming the chat with hate, powered by those temple elites who were low-key terrified of Jesus' influencer status. Pilate, sensing a PR disaster, played the crowd and passed Jesus off to Herod. You know, Herod—the tetrarch with a rep for throwing wild parties and making rash decisions.

Herod was all hyped to meet this miracle man everyone was tweeting about. He thought Jesus would drop some miracle content right there, maybe turn water into wine, or at least float a little. But Jesus wasn't about to perform for this clout chaser. Nope, He kept it muted, no comments, just left Herod on read. Herod's verdict? "This guy's no LOL, send him back to Pilate."

So, Jesus was yeeted back to Pilate, who was now seriously over this episode of "Jerusalem's Most Wanted." In a twist, Pilate pulled out Barabbas—a real bad hombre, notorious bandit and all-around troublemaker—and was like, "Okay, let's make this interactive. Who do you want me to release at your festival—Jesus or Barabbas?" Expecting them to be #TeamJesus.

But nah, the crowd was fully hacked by the chief priests, and they started chanting for Barabbas. It was peak betrayal, the OG cancel culture. They chose a legit criminal over a man whose biggest crime was flipping tables and spitting too much truth.

Pilate, washing his hands of the whole drama fest, was like, "Fine, have it your way. But I'm out." He gave the people what they wanted, freed Barabbas, and handed Jesus over to be crucified. It was a verdict delivered not by justice, but by a mob's trending hashtag: #Crucify.

And that's how Jesus, the man who came to change the world with love and miracles, ended up on the path to the cross—betrayed by a friend, bounced between rulers, and chosen over by a public that once hung on his every parable. The trial was less about law and more about likes, proving that even in ancient times, public opinion could cancel just about anyone.

Top of Form

CHAPTER 6
The Crucifixion: The Ultimate Low

6.1 The Path to Golgotha

So here's how it went down: Jesus, already beat from the trials—literally and figuratively—had to haul His own cross through the streets. This wasn't just any stroll; it was a trek up Golgotha, aka Skull Hill, and the vibe was heavy, with the cross weighing down like the worst kind of burden anyone could DM you.

As Jesus stumbled through the streets, the scene was straight out of a dramatic influencer live-feed. Spectators lined up, some throwing shade with looks that could kill, while others couldn't hide their heartbreak, their eyes streaming more than a viral sad TikTok. Amid the chaos, some tried to offer comfort, like the women of Jerusalem—true ride-or-dies—weeping and wailing out in public, giving realness to the sorrow.

But here's where it gets real: As Jesus was maxing out on His endurance, Simon of Cyrene, just a regular dude minding his own business, gets pulled from the crowd. Roman soldiers were like, "You! Yeah, you! Help Him carry this." And just like that, Simon's thrown into this Insta-worthy moment of suffering, forced to help carry the cross. Lowkey, it was a moment of unexpected solidarity, a random guy sharing the load on this grim journey.

Together, they trudged towards Golgotha, the crowd a mix of haters and heartbreakers, some throwing insults, others silent in their support, all caught up in this intense, real-time drama. The air was thick, not just with the heat of the Middle Eastern sun, but with the weight of what was happening—history in the making, and not the kind you'd double-tap for likes.

Reaching the hill was no relief, as the worst was yet to come. But in that walk, in every step Jesus took towards the place where He'd be crucified, there was this heavy mix of dread and determination, a playlist of pain that would resonate through history. And Simon, part of this story now, wasn't just a face in the crowd anymore. He was part of the path, a symbol of the burden shared, even if just for part of the way.

6.2 The Crucifixion: The Ultimate Low

Now, we've hit the peak of the playlist—Golgotha, where the scene was more intense than any horror flick. Jesus, exhausted and battered, arrives at the ultimate stage of his earthly mission. The air was thick with despair as the soldiers nailed Him to the cross, a spectacle none of his followers could have ever playlisted in their minds.

To His left and right, two thieves were also being crucified, adding to the grim vibe of the scene. It was like a public execution, but with a twist—the man in the middle was being punished not for what He had done but for who He was. Spectators and passersby couldn't help but pause, their usual day interrupted by an extraordinary, unsettling sight. Some jeered, their words sharp as the thorns on Jesus' crown. Others, the silent watchers, their eyes spoke volumes, a mix of confusion, horror, and in some, a deep, mournful understanding.

The disciples? They were there, but just barely. Hovering on the edges, torn between disbelief and despair, their world was crashing. Imagine your entire feed, your whole support system, suddenly flashing the spinning wheel of doom—that was them, buffering in real-time, as their leader and friend hung there.

Above the murmurs of the crowd, Jesus' voice broke through. Despite the unimaginable pain, His words were for others—forgiving the soldiers, addressing His mother Mary and His disciple John with words that formed new bonds, and promising paradise to a repentant thief beside Him. Each statement, heavy with significance, was a tweet that didn't need a character limit to resonate deeply.

As Jesus uttered His last, "It is finished," the sky turned dark as if mourning, the earth shook, and the massive temple veil tore down the middle—like a divine mic drop signaling the enormity of the moment. The crowd was left in a mix of awe and terror; some ran, others knelt, many were just shook.

This wasn't just a physical ordeal; it was an emotional earthquake, shaking the foundations of what the onlookers believed and understood about power, justice, and divinity. It was the kind of event you couldn't just scroll past. It demanded a pause, a deep, soul-shaking pause, to comprehend the gravity of what had just unfolded on that dusty, blood-soaked hill.

6.3 The Last Words: Epic Mic Drops from the Cross

As the sky pulled a major gloom mood and the earth itself felt the vibe check, Jesus, hanging there on the cross, kept dropping truth bombs that resonated deeper than any trending tweet could. His final words were more than just sound bites; they were deep cuts into the heart of humanity, echoing through the chaos at Golgotha like the ultimate playlist for the soul.

"Father, forgive them, for they do not know what they are doing." This plea wasn't just about giving a pass to those nailing Him up; it was a global shoutout for forgiveness that slapped differently, challenging everyone to level up beyond revenge. Even strapped to the cross, Jesus was setting #ForgivenessGoals like a legend.

"I thirst." This shout wasn't just about needing a drink; it symbolized a deep thirst for connection, a raw human moment that showed Jesus wasn't just a divine meme but felt all the feels just like us. It was a vibe that reminded everyone that being parched for something real wasn't a weakness; it was a shared human tweet.

"It is finished." With this drop, Jesus wasn't just clocking out; He was stamping His mission complete. This wasn't your everyday sign-off. This was the divine flex, signaling that the biggest job ever—patching up humanity's relationship with the sky squad—was done and dusted.

"Father, into your hands I commit my spirit." As His last breath faded, the atmosphere was thick with a mix of heartbreak and mystery. At that moment, the temple veil—yeah, that big curtain that kept regular folks from the VIP God zone—ripped top to bottom. No cap, it was like the heavens were tearing up the old rule book right before everyone's eyes. It was the ultimate "seen" receipt from the divine, proving the message was loud and clear.

The blackout vibes that rolled over the land and the dramatic veil tear weren't just for the 'Gram; they were powerful signs that the world was under new management. Everyone from His ride-or-die disciples to the day-one skeptics was hit with a reality where old hashtags died and new trends of hope started trending.

These final epic moments weren't just about dropping mics but dropping barriers, making sacred spaces accessible and spinning a global movement of faith, hope, and epic love. These weren't just words to be heard; they were words to be lived, retweeted through ages, inspiring everyone to not just double-tap on life but truly embrace it.

CHAPTER 7
The Burial

7.1 The Aftermath: When the Feed Went Dark

Post-crucifixion vibes were heavy. As Jesus took His last breath, the whole scene at Golgotha was like the darkest downer, straight-up shadow-banning any light. Nature itself couldn't handle the tea; the sky went full-on do not disturb mode, and the earth shook like it just dropped its entire follower count.

Right there, as Jesus hung lifeless, a Roman soldier, part of the squad meant to keep the peace, stepped up for a vibe check. He needed to confirm the death—standard procedure but heavy all the same. With a spear, he gave a final poke, and bam, it was clear: Jesus wasn't faking it for the 'Gram. This was the real deal, death confirmed, no respawns. The soldier, caught up in the moment, was like, "Truly, this man was the Son of God." Even he couldn't scroll past this without dropping a serious truth bomb.

Meanwhile, the crowd that had gathered was beginning to disperse, their content thirst quenched but their spirits low. Some were ghosting the scene, shook and silent. Others were buzzing with what-ifs and hot takes, their minds racing faster than their data speeds. It was a major plot twist no one had on their bingo card.

As the sun began to dip, signaling the DM slide into the Sabbath, things needed to move quickly. No one wanted to catch heat for breaking rules, especially not with the eyes of the Roman mods on them. The next steps were crucial, and time was ticking faster than a Snapchat streak.

7.2 Joseph of Arimathea and the Tomb: The Last-Minute Save

Enter Joseph of Arimathea, total low-key hero of the hour. This dude was not just a secret admirer of Jesus' teachings but also a VIP in the council with some serious clout. With the Sabbath countdown popping off, Joseph wasn't about to let Jesus' body just hang out without proper respects. No way, not on his watch.

Joseph, being the boss that he is, rolls up to Pilate's DMs with a bold ask. He's like, "Yo, can I take Jesus' body down? Big Sabbath energy coming, and we need to wrap this up, literally." Pilate, probably still shook from the day's drama, hits him with the blue check—permission granted.

With the clock ticking faster than a TikTok timer, Joseph books it over to Golgotha. He's on a mission, backed up by Nicodemus, another undercover Jesus fan, who comes through clutch with a mixtape of myrrh and aloes—about seventy-five pounds of burial spice. Talk about setting the bar high for funeral goals.

Together, they get Jesus down from the cross, handling Him with more care than a limited-edition sneaker drop. They wrap Him up in linen—fresh out the box—like they're packaging a high-end collectible, only this time it's out of reverence, not resale. These guys were giving Jesus the VIP treatment, all while the Sabbath was loading, making every second count.

They hustle to a new tomb, which was like the latest drop in prime real estate, never used, and just waiting for such a moment. With the sun dipping and the Sabbath basically on their doorstep, they slide Jesus into the tomb, roll a big ol' stone across the entrance like they're locking down the most exclusive drop of the century, and it's game over.

Joseph and Nicodemus, exhausted but relieved, step back. They've just pulled off the ultimate Sabbath prep, ensuring Jesus rests in peace while everyone else hits pause for the holy day. It was a burial fit for a king, done in haste but packed with all the honors they could muster in the nick of time.

CHAPTER 8
The Resurrection: The Legendary Comeback

8.1 The Discovery: Tomb Unlocked, Jesus Gone

Alright, so it was early morning vibes, and Mary Magdalene along with her squad of loyal ladies were heading to the tomb. They were rolling up with spices to keep things fresh, thinking they'd have to deal with a big ol' rock blocking their way. But nah, they arrived and boom—plot twist—the stone was already yeeted aside. Like, someone had straight-up ghosted it from the entrance.

They peek inside, and it's giving total empty vibes. No Jesus, just linens lying there like the aftermath of a sold-out drop where everything's been snatched up. The women were shook—like, where did their main guy go? Was this some kind of spiritual restock? The scene was more baffling than finding out your favorite influencer just went private out of nowhere.

This wasn't just a missing body situation; it was the kind of mystery that had them double-checking if they were at the right spot. Imagine showing up to a concert, and the venue is just...empty. No signs, no nothing. Just vibes and confusion.

So there they were, lowkey freaking out, wondering if they'd just walked into the most epic plot twist of their lives. Little did they know, they were about to get the news drop of the century that was about to turn their world from "seen" to "unbelievable."

8.2 The Angelic Message: Heavenly Drop of the Hottest News

Just as the squad was trying to process the empty tomb vibe, the morning threw them another curveball. Out of nowhere, it's like a scene straight from a divine influencer's story—there's this angel posted up where Jesus had been laid. We're talking about an angel with a glow so bright, it was like the OG ring light had just been turned on. The vibes were celestial, the aesthetic otherworldly.

The angel hits them with the headline drop of eternity: "He is not here; He has risen, just as He said." This wasn't just good news; it was the kind of epic update that flips the whole script. Jesus wasn't just missing; He had leveled up beyond death itself.

The women's reactions? A wild mix of hype and horror, their emotions doing the full TikTok 10-second challenge—fear, joy, disbelief, all rolled into one. It was like getting the notification of your life, but the message is so fire, you can't help but question if it's real.

"Don't be afraid," the angel continued, probably seeing their faces were a mix of 'OMG' and 'WTF'. "Go quickly and tell His disciples, 'He has risen from the dead and is going ahead of you into Galilee. There you will see Him.' Now that's what I call a comeback season!"

And just like that, the women were turned into the first messengers of the resurrection, tasked with spreading a story so lit, it was bound to go viral. With hearts pounding like they just dropped the hottest gossip of the millennium, they dashed off, ready to spill the celestial tea to the disciples. This angelic encounter wasn't just a meeting; it was the ultimate reveal party, and they had front-row tickets.

8. 3 Appearances: The Ultimate Encore Performances

Post-angelic drop, Jesus wasn't about to keep His comeback low-key. Nah, He went full-on tour mode, making surprise appearances that had everyone shook. First up, Mary Magdalene, who was out here trying to process the empty tomb. When she saw Jesus, she didn't even clock it was Him—thought He was the gardener! Talk about mistaken identity. But when He dropped her name, "Mary," it hit different. Suddenly, it was clear. This wasn't just some rando; it was Jesus, back like He never left!

Next, Jesus took His encore to the road to Emmaus. Two disciples were just walking, debriefing all the recent drama, when Jesus rolled up incognito. He started breaking down the scriptures, serving up insights like a seasoned influencer. It wasn't until He broke bread later that the mic dropped—they realized it was Jesus all along, giving them the ultimate mind-blown moment. But quick as a swipe, He ghosted them, leaving them amazed and tweeting with their feet back to Jerusalem to spread the word.

But Jesus wasn't done. He had a main event planned, a group hang with all the disciples. He popped up in their locked room like, "Peace be with you." No doorbell, no knocking, just straight up appearing. If their minds weren't already blown, they were now. Jesus showed them the wounds, the real marks of His journey, just to prove this wasn't some lookalike challenge—it was Him, 100%.

The squad was all kinds of emotional—joy, disbelief, wonder. This appearance was more than just a reunion; it was proof that their leader, their friend, wasn't just back for a limited run. He was showing them the real deal—He had conquered death, and this comeback tour was about to change everything.

And like that, Jesus not only cemented His status as the ultimate comeback king but also set the stage for His followers to turn the world upside down. With each appearance, He was writing history's greatest sequel, live and direct.

CHAPTER 9
The Implications of the Resurrection

9.1 The Ripple Effect: Spreading the Ultimate Comeback Story

So here's the sitch: when word got out that Jesus wasn't just back, but He'd straight-up conquered death, the news spread faster than a viral dance challenge. This wasn't just some whispered rumor in back alleys; it was the headline everyone needed to hear. His followers were hyped, their faith levels hitting new peaks—Jesus had truly done the impossible, and now they were all witnesses.

But this wasn't just a win for the home team. The religious leaders and Roman bigwigs? Yeah, they were sweating. This resurrection business threw a mega wrench into their plans. They'd hoped the crucifixion was the mic drop to end all challenges to their authority. Instead, Jesus' comeback was like hitting the refresh button on His whole movement. Now, His followers weren't just mourning a loss; they were mobilizing an uprising.

The buzz around Jesus' resurrection was more disruptive than a surprise album drop at midnight. It had people rethinking everything they thought they knew about power, authority, and what's possible. And let's not forget the squad—Jesus' disciples. They went from confused and shook to bold and empowered. They were out there, spreading the news, no longer just followers but leaders, influencers in their own right, armed with a truth that couldn't be silenced.

This ripple effect was turning tides. It wasn't just about a miracle; it was about movement. The higher-ups tried to clamp down, but the word was out and spreading like wildfire. Every testimony, every shared story was like another post going viral, building a network of believers tuned into a message of hope and transformation. This was the kind of organic reach marketers dream of, and it was all powered by the most epic comeback in history.

9.2 The Great Commission: Dropping the Ultimate Collab Invite

After the shockwave of His epic resurrection moment, Jesus wasn't about to ghost His crew. Nah, He had a major meet-up, one that was about to set the stage for the next level of their journey. So, when He rolled up to the disciples, it wasn't just for a reunion—it was to drop the ultimate collab invite.

He gathered His squad and was like, "Look, fam, all authority in heaven and on Earth has been given to ya boy. Now, I'm passing the mic to you." This was the big moment—the Great Commission. Jesus was telling them to go all out, to spread the vibe from their local hood to the ends of the earth, making disciples of all nations. It was like He was setting up His own viral challenge, but this one was about changing lives, not just racking up views.

And Jesus wasn't just about tossing this massive task their way without backup. He promised them the Holy Spirit, the ultimate hype man, would be coming through to empower them. This was like getting the best backstage pass ever because with the Holy Spirit, they'd have the power to keep the momentum going, to heal, preach, and live out the hype Jesus started.

"Baptize them in the name of the Father, the Son, and the Holy Spirit. Teach 'em all I've commanded you," He continued. And for the real kicker, He added, "And yo, remember, I'm with you, always, to the very end of the age." That's the kind of squad goals Jesus was setting.

This wasn't just a farewell; it was a commencement. The disciples were being turned from followers into leaders, from listeners into speakers, from the audience into headliners. The Great Commission was their call to keep the party going, to keep spreading the Jesus vibes across continents and generations. With this divine shoutout, they were ready to make waves, backed by the promise that the main man Himself was still in their corner, no matter what.

9.3 The Ascension: Jesus Hits the Ultimate Upvote

After laying down the ultimate game plan with the Great Commission, Jesus wasn't about to just fade into the background like some one-hit-wonder. Nah, He had one more show-stopping move up His sleeve. Gathered with His squad for what seemed like another chill hangout, Jesus suddenly took things to the next level—literally.

As they were all vibing, Jesus started levitating, pulling the most epic levitate challenge ever. He was ascending, floating up into the sky like He was on some ultra-exclusive celestial elevator. The disciples were just standing there, jaws dropped, phones out (if they had them), capturing this mind-blowing moment. Jesus was going full cloud surfer, rising higher until He was nothing but a speck in the sky.

And just like that, He was gone, out of sight but never out of mind. It was the ascension, the ultimate mic drop and cloud pop combined. The disciples were left there, probably thinking, "Did that just really happen?" But this wasn't just a party trick; it was the sign-off that sealed the deal on Jesus' earth tour.

Left gazing up into the sky, the disciples were probably feeling a mix of hype and heartache, but then—plot twist—two angels popped up in some fresh white gear and were like, "Yo, why you still looking up? This isn't the end; it's just the intermission. He'll be back like your favorite series reboot."

So, with that celestial cameo, the disciples knew it was time to get moving. Jesus' ascension wasn't just a farewell; it was a signal to start spreading the word, to kick off the global tour of love, faith, and salvation. They hit the ground running, fueled by the Holy Spirit and the ultimate promise that their leader, mentor, and friend would one day make a comeback.

The ascension set the stage for the spread of Christianity, turning a ragtag group of followers into founders of a movement that would rack up followers in numbers they couldn't even fathom. Jesus' life, death, and resurrection weren't just past tense; they were the blueprint for the future, a viral legacy that would trend across centuries.

CHAPTER 10
Reflection

10.1 Legacy and Faith: Jesus, The Ultimate Trendsetter

Let's unpack this—Jesus was more than just a historical figure; He was the ultimate trendsetter, launching a whole new era of spiritual clout. His days on Earth were a masterclass in flipping the script—turning ordinary moments into viral teachings and humble gatherings into lessons on love and justice that have been hitting different for over two millennia.

Imagine this dude, a carpenter turned radical influencer, dropping truth bombs like "Blessed are the meek" and "Love your enemies"— content so fire it's been quoted, reposted, and lived out across generations. These weren't just throwaway posts; they were deep, transformational vibes that continue to challenge and inspire.

His crucifixion? That was the darkest plot twist, but then He hit us with the ultimate comeback—His resurrection. This wasn't just a season finale cliffhanger; it sparked a global fandom, a movement of people vibing with His message of hope and redemption, turning that epic comeback story into a lifestyle.

Reflecting on Jesus' legacy is like checking the ultimate influencer's feed where every post breaks the internet. His influence keeps trending, not just in liturgies but in real-life actions—charity, compassion, radical forgiveness. That's the kind of content that doesn't just get likes; it changes lives. He's not just a figure from the past; He's the blueprint for kindness, courage, and community that keeps slaying in the hearts of billions, proving that some influencers are timeless, and their hashtags never fade.

10. 2 Modern-Day Relevance: Jesus' Message Still Slaps

Alright, let's dive into why Jesus' vibes are still relevant and why His message slaps even today. The themes of sacrifice, redemption, and hope? They're not just ancient history—they're straight-up life goals for us, even in the 21st century. Let's break it down.

Sacrifice: Jesus' ultimate flex was giving up His life for the greater good. In a world where it's all about me, me, me, His selfless act is a whole mood. Think about it: in a time where we're constantly trying to level up, secure the bag, and glow up, His sacrifice reminds us that sometimes the biggest wins come from the most selfless plays. It's the original act of paying it forward.

Redemption: We all mess up—no cap. But Jesus' story of redemption is like the ultimate comeback narrative. He took our L's, flipped them into lessons, and showed us that it's never too late to turn things around. This is the kind of content that hits different because it's relatable. It's the reassurance that no matter how many times we stumble, we can always bounce back, stronger and better.

Hope: In a world full of low-key anxiety and high-key chaos, Jesus' message of hope is the anchor we need. His resurrection is the ultimate plot twist that promises things can and will get better. It's like that light at the end of a never-ending tunnel, the ultimate glow-up. It's the kind of promise that keeps us going, reminding us that there's always a reason to hold on and keep pushing forward.

Today's world is a wild ride, full of ups and downs, but Jesus' teachings are the OG guide to navigating it all. His message is still the blueprint for living a life that's full of meaning and purpose. Whether you're facing your own trials, dealing with betrayal, or just trying to find your way, His themes of sacrifice, redemption, and hope are timeless truths that resonate. They're the cheat codes to a life that's more than just surviving—it's about thriving, with faith and purpose guiding the way.

So, even in our fast-paced, swipe-left, swipe-right culture, Jesus' message remains a major key. It's the kind of wisdom that's always on trend, providing the inspo we need to keep our heads up and our hearts open.

Conclusion: Your Turn to Influence

Alright fam, we've taken a wild ride through the ultimate comeback story—Jesus' life, teachings, and epic plot twists. From His birth in the most low-key but lit way possible to His legendary resurrection, every part of Jesus' journey has been dropping major inspo for over two thousand years. His teachings weren't just lit back in the day; they're still the ultimate life hacks for today.

Reflecting on Jesus' Impact: Jesus was the OG influencer who set the trend for radical love, unshakeable hope, and next-level faith. He wasn't just about talk; He was about action, walking the walk even when it led to the cross. His sacrifices and lessons are still the blueprint for living a life that's more than just flexing on the 'gram— it's about making real, lasting changes in the world. His story is like a never-ending thread of epic content that continues to inspire, challenge, and empower.

Your Call to Action: Now, here's where you come in. Jesus showed us how to live with purpose, love without limits, and spread vibes that uplift and unite. Gen Z, it's your turn to take that baton and run with it. You're already pros at influencing trends and sparking movements, so why not channel that same energy into living out the teachings of Jesus? Be the change-makers, the hope-bringers, the ones who show up with love and light in every space you enter.

Be Influencers in Your Own Right: Just like Jesus flipped the script in His time, you can do the same today. Whether it's through acts of kindness, standing up for justice, or simply being a beacon of positivity, you have the power to make a difference. Let Jesus' story be the ultimate guide to how you can live your best life—one that's full of purpose, impact, and endless good vibes.

So, go out there and slay, fam. Spread the love, share the hope, and keep the faith alive. Jesus' legacy is in your hands now, and with your unique flair and unstoppable spirit, you can keep His message trending for generations to come. Remember, you're not just followers; you're leaders, influencers, and game-changers. Let's keep this movement going, one lit act of love at a time. #JesusVibes #GenZInfluence

Appendices:

Glossary of Terms

AF: An very loose acronym for "as heck," used for emphasis. Example: "That concert was lit AF!"

Amped: Excited. Example: "I'm amped for the concert tonight!"

Ate: Delivered something exceptionally well. Example: "She ate that performance!"

Bae: Boyfriend or girlfriend. Example: "Wait, bae is calling me."

Basic: Someone unoriginal and only interested in popular things. Example: "She's so basic with her pumpkin spice latte."

Bet: In agreement or affirmative. Example: "Want to come over? Bet!"

Big Yikes: Very embarrassing or cringey. Example: "That singing audition didn't go as he planned…big yikes."

Blessed: Feeling fortunate or grateful. Example: "I'm so blessed to have great friends."

Boujee/Bougie: Fancy or luxurious. Example: "The hotel was so boujee!"

Bruh: Used to express shock or disappointment. Example: "Bruh, what you did was not cool."

Bussin': Really good. Example: "This burrito is bussin'!"

Cap/No Cap: Lying or faking; No cap means telling the truth. Example: "I actually went to class today. No cap."

CEO: Master or expert of something. Example: "You came first again! You're the CEO of that game."

Clout: Fame or popularity within social media. Example: "He's built good clout with 1 million followers on Instagram."

Delulu: Short for delusional, used for irrational beliefs. Example: "He smiled at me, he must like me. You're being delulu."

Dip: To leave suddenly. Example: "I'm about to dip."

Dope: Exceptional or awesome. Example: "That bike is dope!"

Drip: Stylish appearance. Example: "You got drip with those new shoes."

Dub: Short for W, meaning win. Example: "We took the dub."

Extra: Overly excessive or dramatic. Example: "That whole wedding was super extra."

Fam: Friends, colleagues, or anyone who feels like family. Example: "It's okay fam, we'll get through this."

Finna: Fixing to, or going to. Example: "I'm finna go to the mall."

Fire: Amazing or exciting. Example: "That waterslide is fire!"

Flex: To flaunt or brag about something. Example: "He's flexing with those kicks."

Gassed/Gassing: Exaggerating someone's abilities or accomplishments. Example: "She's already confident enough, she doesn't need any more gassing."

Ghosted: Cutting off communication with someone with no explanation. Example: "After a couple of weeks of texting, he suddenly ghosted me."

Glow-up: A major transformation in appearance. Example: "She had a glow-up. She looks great!"

GOAT: Greatest of all time. Example: "My coach is the GOAT!"

Gyat: Expression of admiration. Example: "Gyat! Those jeans make you look so good!"

High key: Overt or obvious. Example: "I high key love that new movie."

Hits different: Special or unique. Example: "My mom's cooking just hits different."

Ick: Feeling of disgust. Example: "Did you see how mean he was to his little brother? That's such an ick."

IJBOL: Acronym for "I just burst out laughing." Example: "You're hilarious, IJBOL."

It's giving: Describes the vibe or connotation of something. Example: "Her outfit is giving 90s fashion."

IYKYK: Acronym for "If you know, you know." Example: "The ski trip was wild! IYKYK."

Lit: Exciting, excellent, or intoxicated. Example: "The movie was lit!"

Low key: Keep a low profile. Example: "I low key am so keen for the concert on Saturday."

Menty b: Short for mental breakdown. Example: "I've had multiple menty b's this week."

Mid: Average or not great. Example: "That show was mid."

No cap: Not lying. Example: "I'm so happy for you, no cap."

OMG: Acronym for "Oh my God." Example: "OMG, I can't believe you just said that!"

OMW: Acronym for "On my way." Example: "OMW! I'll be there in 20."

Periodt: Emphasizes the finality of a statement. Example: "We're not going back. Periodt."

Rizz: Short for charisma. Example: "He's got so much rizz."

Salty: Upset or irritated. Example: "They're just salty because they're jealous."

Simp: Someone who does too much for someone they're interested in. Example: "Look at him, following her like a puppy. He's such a simp."

Slaps: Something that is really good. Example: "This pizza slaps."

Slay: Doing something extremely well. Example: "She slayed that song!"

Smol: Small in a cute way. Example: "Ah…he's so smol."

Squad: Group of friends. Example: "Hanging out with the squad tonight."

Stan: Overzealous fan. Example: "She's a huge stan of Taylor Swift."

Sus: Short for suspicious. Example: "She's acting really sus."

Tea: Gossip. Example: "Are you going to spill the tea or what?"

Thirsty: Desperate for attention. Example: "She's so thirsty—look at all the Instagram stories she's posted."

Vibes: Feelings or atmosphere. Example: "I love your whole vibe."

Vibe check: Checking one's attitude or personality. Example: "You need a vibe check."

Yeet: To throw something forcefully. Example: "He yeeted that pencil across the classroom!"

Zaddy: Handsome, fashionable older man. Example: "She found a zaddy as soon as she graduated."

Discussion Questions

1. **General Reflections:**

   • What were your overall impressions of "The O.G. Influencer: Gospel Stories for Gen Z"? Which story resonated with you the most and why?

2. **Slang and Accessibility:**

   • How did the use of Gen Z slang affect your understanding and engagement with the stories? Did it make the content more relatable and accessible to you?

3. **Character Analysis:**

   • How are the disciples portrayed in a way that makes them relatable to today's audience? Which disciple do you find most interesting or inspiring?

4. **Modern Parallels:**

   • What modern situations can you relate to the parables and miracles described in the book? How can you apply these lessons in your own life?

5. **Cultural Relevance:**

   • How does this modern retelling of the Gospel stories highlight the cultural relevance of Jesus' teachings for today's world?

6. **Themes of Sacrifice and Redemption:**

   - Discuss the themes of sacrifice, redemption, and hope in the context of Gen Z culture. How do these themes resonate with contemporary issues and challenges?

7. **Role of Humor:**

   - How did the humor and light-hearted tone impact your reading experience? Do you think it helped in conveying the messages more effectively?

8. **Faith and Doubt:**

   - How does the book address the concepts of faith and doubt? Do you feel it provides a fresh perspective on handling these aspects in your own spiritual journey?

9. **Influence and Impact:**

   - Reflect on how Jesus' life and teachings have influenced the world historically and continue to impact people today. How do you see yourself contributing to this legacy?

10. **Community and Action:**

    - How can you apply the call to action from this book in your community? What are some practical steps you can take to embody the teachings of Jesus in your daily life?

11. **Favorite Moments:**

    - Share your favorite moments or quotes from the book. Why did these stand out to you?

12. **Critical Perspective:**

- Were there any parts of the book you found challenging or difficult to understand? How did you navigate these sections?

13. **Future Retellings:**

- How would you like to see other parts of the Bible or religious texts retold in a similar style? Are there specific stories or books you think would benefit from a modern, slang-filled adaptation?

14. **Personal Growth:**

- In what ways has reading this book impacted your personal growth and spiritual understanding? Can you identify any changes in your perspective or behavior since engaging with the text?

15. **Creative Expression:**

- How would you creatively express one of the stories or teachings from this book? Consider writing, art, music, or another medium. Share your ideas with the group.

Further Reading: Resources for More Traditional Interpretations and Further Study

1. **The Holy Bible:**

   - **New International Version (NIV):** A popular and widely accepted modern English translation.

   - **King James Version (KJV):** Known for its majestic style and poetic language, a classic choice for traditional study.

   - **New Revised Standard Version (NRSV):** Preferred by many scholars for its balance of readability and accuracy.

2. **Commentaries:**

   - **"Matthew Henry's Commentary on the Whole Bible":** A comprehensive and detailed classic commentary, providing verse-by-verse insights.

   - **"The New Bible Commentary" by D.A. Carson, R.T. France, J.A. Motyer, and Gordon J. Wenham:** A one-volume commentary covering the entire Bible with scholarly insights.

   - **"The Expositor's Bible Commentary" edited by Frank E. Gaebelein:** A multi-volume series offering in-depth commentary and analysis.

3. **Study Bibles:**

   - **"The NIV Study Bible":** Offers detailed notes, cross-references, and introductions to each book of the Bible.

- **"The ESV Study Bible":** Known for its comprehensive notes, maps, and articles, providing a deep dive into biblical texts.

- **"The Life Application Study Bible":** Focuses on practical application of biblical principles to daily life.

4. **Books on Jesus' Life and Teachings:**

- **"The Case for Christ" by Lee Strobel:** An investigative journalist examines the historical evidence for Jesus.

- **"Jesus: A Pilgrimage" by James Martin, SJ:** Combines biblical scholarship, historical research, and personal reflections.

- **"Simply Jesus: A New Vision of Who He Was, What He Did, and Why He Matters" by N.T. Wright:** Explores the historical and theological significance of Jesus.

5. **Books on the Gospels:**

- **"Four Portraits, One Jesus: A Survey of Jesus and the Gospels" by Mark L. Strauss:** A comprehensive introduction to the Gospels and their unique perspectives on Jesus.

- **"Jesus and the Gospels: An Introduction and Survey" by Craig L. Blomberg:** Provides an overview of the historical and literary contexts of the Gospels.

- **"The Gospel of Matthew: A Commentary" by R.T. France:** An in-depth analysis of the Gospel of Matthew.

6. **Historical Context:**

   - **"The Historical Jesus: The Life of a Mediterranean Jewish Peasant" by John Dominic Crossan:** Examines the historical context and life of Jesus.

   - **"Jesus and the Eyewitnesses: The Gospels as Eyewitness Testimony" by Richard Bauckham:** Argues for the reliability of the Gospels based on eyewitness accounts.

   - **"The Jewish Annotated New Testament" edited by Amy-Jill Levine and Marc Zvi Brettler:** Provides insights into the Jewish context of the New Testament.

7. **Bible Study Tools:**

   - **"Strong's Exhaustive Concordance of the Bible":** An essential tool for in-depth word study and cross-referencing.

   - **"Vine's Complete Expository Dictionary of Old and New Testament Words":** Helps understand the original meanings of biblical terms.

   - **"Bible Gateway"** (www.biblegateway.com): An online resource offering multiple translations, commentaries, and study tools.

8. **Theological Perspectives:**

   - **"Systematic Theology" by Wayne Grudem:** A comprehensive guide to Christian theology.

   - **"Knowing God" by J.I. Packer:** Explores the nature of God and the relationship believers can have with Him.

- **"The Cost of Discipleship" by Dietrich Bonhoeffer:** A classic work on the meaning of Christian discipleship.

These resources provide a range of traditional interpretations and scholarly insights to deepen your understanding and study of the Bible and the life of Jesus.

Made in the USA
Las Vegas, NV
19 December 2024

14912639R00059